Canada Close Up

# Newfoundland and Labrador

### Rachel Eagen

D0898827

## Scholastic Canada Ltd.

Toronto  New York  London  Auckland  Sydney
Mexico City  New Delhi  Hong Kong  Buenos Aires

**Visual Credits:**

Cover: Dale Wilson ©AllCanadaPhotos.com; p. I: Danita Delimont/Alamy; p. III: All Canada Photos/Alamy; p. IV: Joe Gough/Shutterstock Inc. (right); Rolf Hicker Photography/Alamy (top left), Mirka Moksha/Shutterstock Inc. (bottom left); p. 2: Matthew Collingwood/Shutterstock Inc.; p. 4: Yva Momatiuk & John Eastcott/Momdem Pictures/National Geographic Stock; p. 5: JOHN EASTCOTT AND YVA MOMATIUK/National Geographic Stock; p. 7: RICHARD OLSENIUS/National Geographic Stock; p. 8 and back cover: Near and Far Photography/Shutterstock Inc.; p. 10: AioK/Shutterstock Inc.; p. 11: Eric Isselée/Shutterstock Inc. (bottom left), David Noton Photography/Alamy (top), Pixshots/Shutterstock Inc. (bottom right); p. 12: Barrett & MacKay ©AllCanadaPhotos.com; p. 13: Mary Evans Picture Library/MARK FURNESS; p. 14: Claude Bouchard/First Light (behind), Library and Archives Canada, Acc. No. 1977-14-1 (top); p. 15: Bryan & Cherry Alexander Photography/Alamy (top), FloridaStock/Shutterstock Inc. (bottom); p. 16: North Wind Picture Archives/Alamy (top), Rolf Hicker Photography/Alamy (bottom); p. 17: The Rooms Provincial Archives, F 50-6; p. 18: Mary Evans Picture Library/MARY EVANS ILN PICTURES; p. 19: K. Bruce Lane Photography; p. 21: Duncan Cameron/Library and Archives Canada/PA-113253; p. 22: Rolf Hicker/AllCanadaPhotos.com; p. 23: Barrett & MacKay ©AllCanadaPhotos.com; p. 24: Bart Goossens/Shutterstock Inc.; p. 25: Rolf Hicker/AllCanadaPhotos.com; p. 26: Pete Ryan/National Geographic Stock; p. 27: THE CANADIAN PRESS/Adrian Wyld; p. 28: David L. Blackwood, *William Lane Leaving Bragg's Island*, 1971, The Rooms Provincial Art Gallery, Memorial University of Newfoundland Collection (top), Mary Evans Picture Library (bottom); p. 29: Aga & Miko (arsat)/Shutterstock Inc. (top), The Canadian Press/St. John's Telegram - Gary Hebbard (bottom); p. 30: Terese Loeb Kreuzer/Alamy; p. 31: CP PHOTO/St. John's Telegram - Joe Gibbons; p. 32: Barrett & MacKay © AllCanadaPhotos.com (bottom), John Sylvester © AllCanadaPhotos.com (top); p. 33: Dorling Kindersley (bottom), John Eastcott and Yva Momatiuk/National Geographic Stock (top); p. 34: Greg Locke/First Light; p. 35: Toronto Star/First Light; p. 36: AndreyTTL/Shutterstock Inc., Ingram Publishing/SuperStock (middle), Ostromec/Shutterstock Inc. (middle); p. 37: Sam Abell/National Geographic Stock; p. 38: Bruce Amos/Shutterstock Inc.; p. 39: Bettmann/Corbis; p. 40: Sam Abell/National Geographic Stock; p. 41: Maritime History Museum; p. 42: Barrett & MacKay ©AllCanadaPhotos.com (top), Mary Evans Picture Library/Douglas McCarthy (bottom); p. 43: Sean White ©AllCanadaPhotos.com (bottom).

Produced by Plan B Book Packagers
Editorial: Ellen Rodger
Design: Rosie Gowsell-Pattison
Special thanks to consultant and editor Terrance Cox, adjunct professor, Brock University; Tanya Rutledge; Alexandra Cormier; Jim Chernishenko; and Tank O'Hara for her little nuggets of wisdom.

**Library and Archives Canada Cataloguing in Publication**
Eagen, Rachel, 1979-
Newfoundland and Labrador/Rachel Eagen.
(Canada close up)
ISBN 978-0-545-98906-0
1. Newfoundland and Labrador--Juvenile literature.
I. Title. II. Series: Canada close up (Toronto, Ont.)
FC2161.2.E34 2009          j971.8          C2008-906813-0

ISBN-10 0-545-98906-X

6 5 4 3 2 1          Printed in Canada          09 10 11 12 13 14

# Contents

Newfoundland and Labrador's official flower is the purple pitcher plant.

The official bird is the Atlantic puffin.

The provincial gemstone is labradorite.

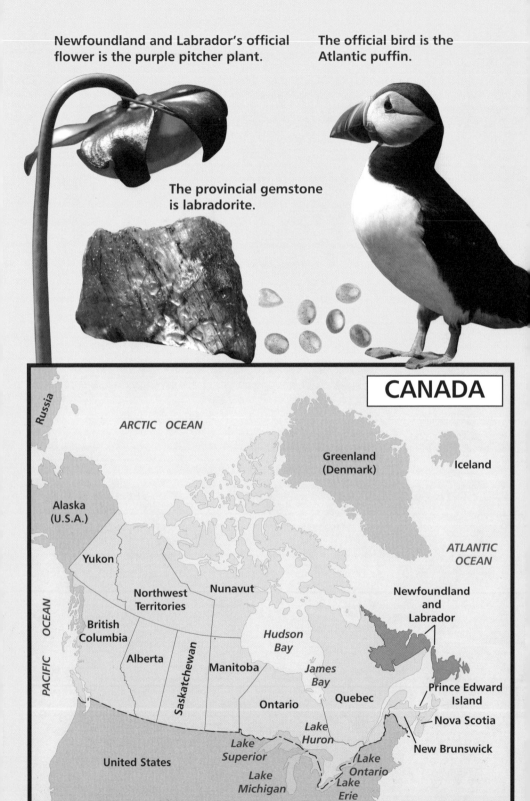

# CANADA

Russia

ARCTIC OCEAN

Greenland (Denmark)

Iceland

Alaska (U.S.A.)

Yukon

ATLANTIC OCEAN

PACIFIC OCEAN

Northwest Territories

Nunavut

Newfoundland and Labrador

British Columbia

Hudson Bay

Alberta

Saskatchewan

Manitoba

James Bay

Quebec

Prince Edward Island

Ontario

Nova Scotia

Lake Huron

New Brunswick

United States

Lake Superior

Lake Michigan

Lake Ontario

Lake Erie

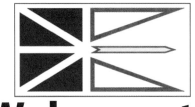

# Welcome to Newfoundland and Labrador!

Newfoundland and Labrador is a province of rock and sea. Stark beauty and harsh conditions are part of everyday life for the 500,000 people who live here. Labradorians and Newfoundlanders are separated by water but they share a mighty spirit and a determined will.

Newfoundland is as far east as you can live in Canada. Pronounced "Noofn-LANd," the island is fondly called "The Rock" by its residents. Its history has been determined by the Atlantic Ocean that surrounds it. Labrador, to the northwest, is a rugged and beautiful part of the Canadian mainland. It covers an area the size of the entire country of New Zealand. "Get on the go," as Newfoundlanders say, and find out more about this great province!

The channel that links St. John's Harbour with the Atlantic Ocean was nicknamed Le Goulet, or The Throat, by French fishermen who came to the region 500 years ago. It is now known as The Narrows.

# Chapter 1
# Rock and Fog

The landscape of Newfoundland and Labrador is jagged and rocky. Millions of years ago, **glaciers** gouged the east coast of Canada, scouring large tracts of land. Thin soils and a harsh climate make it difficult for plants to survive in many parts of the province. On the coasts, sheer cliffs jut upwards from the Atlantic Ocean, giving way to vast **plateaus** throughout the interior.

The province of Newfoundland and Labrador includes two major regions: the island of Newfoundland, and Labrador, which is part of the Canadian mainland. It is the largest Atlantic province. The island is the most eastern part of Canada, and is 111,390 square kilometres in size. Labrador is almost three times the size of Newfoundland, at 294,330 square kilometres.

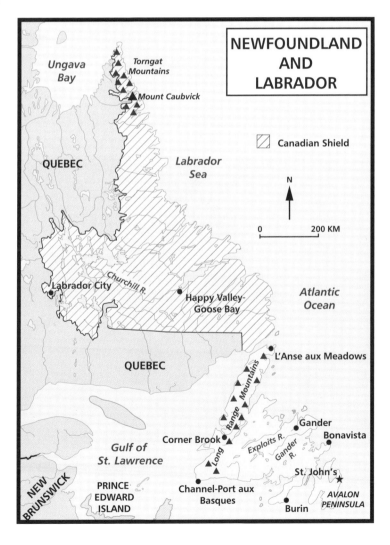

# Shield and mountains

The province includes two major rock formations. The Long Range Mountains cut across Newfoundland. They are the northernmost section of the Appalachian mountain chain. The Canadian Shield stretches across mainland Labrador. This is an important geological rock formation because it is rich in minerals. Northern Labrador has a subarctic climate with short summers and long winters. Forests of spruce, balsam and birch and meadows with lichens and shrubs grow throughout the rest of Labrador.

The Torngat Mountains in northern Labrador include Mount Caubvick, the province's highest peak at 1652 metres.

Tails up! Two humpback whales surprise a windsurfer in the waters of Bonavista Bay, where whales come to feed on the northeast coast.

## Avalon and beyond

The Avalon Peninsula is the most populated area of the province. It extends out into the Atlantic Ocean from the southeastern edge of Newfoundland. Cape Spear, the most easterly point of North America, is located here.

St. John's, the province's bustling capital and the oldest English-founded city in North America, is on the Avalon Peninsula. It is also the most easterly city in North America.

Northwest of the Avalon is the Bonavista Peninsula, famous for spectacular ocean views. In the summer, people come here to spot humpback whales and watch icebergs float past. To the southwest, the Burin Peninsula dangles into the Cabot Strait.

The Great Northern Peninsula on the west side of the island thrusts north, close to mainland Labrador. More than 1000 years ago, Vikings built a settlement here at L'Anse aux Meadows.

## Hills and greens

The rest of Newfoundland is a plateau. This means the land is raised high above the ocean, and stretches out with gently rolling hills. Swampy peat bogs and marshes are found inland. Most of the province is covered in trees that are well suited to the cold, wet climate. Balsam fir, black spruce and pine trees thrive here. Thousands of lakes and streams dot the landscape, but there are only a few major rivers. They include the Exploits and the Gander on the island. The Churchill River runs east across Labrador.

In spring and summer, icebergs float south down the coast on the Labrador Current. These hulking masses of ice break off from the coast of Greenland every spring.

# Weather Makers

Two major ocean **currents** influence the weather in Newfoundland and Labrador. The icy Labrador Current flows south along the east coast of Labrador and on to the Grand Banks of Newfoundland. Here it meets up with the warmer Gulf Stream. Together they create enormous banks of fog.

The interior of Labrador has a subarctic climate. Summers are short and winters are long and very cold. Coastal Labrador has a climate much like on the island. Rain, fog and snow are common in winter. Summers bring more sun and less wind.

# City and outport

Newfoundland and Labrador is a province of small towns and even smaller villages. Some places can't be reached by roads. Visitors to some Labrador communities have to fly in. On the coast of Newfoundland and Labrador, there are still a few old fishing communities where boats are more common than cars!

(left) Fog settles over a fishing village.

There are only a few major cities in the province. The capital city, St. John's, is the most populated with about 100,000 people. Corner Brook is the biggest city on the west coast of the island. Happy Valley–Goose Bay in central Labrador is, with 8000 people, Labrador's largest community.

**Colourfully painted houses line a street in St. John's.**

# Animal tales

Six moose were brought to Newfoundland from Nova Scotia and New Brunswick in 1878 and 1904. It was hoped that they would multiply and provide a source of meat for people on the island. Today, there are more than 120,000 moose – so many that people are warned not to drive at night, to avoid collisions on the roads.

Two much-loved dog breeds come from the province. The Newfoundland is a huge, black, long-haired dog with webbed feet. This strong swimmer can be trained to rescue drowning people. The friendly Labrador retriever is one of the most popular dogs in North America. The breed developed from the dogs that helped fishermen pull their nets ashore.

Several bird species pack the Witless Bay Ecological Reserve, four islands just south of St. John's. More than 260,000 pairs of Atlantic puffins nest here – the largest colony in North America!

Historic re-enactors at L'Anse aux Meadows demonstrate how the Vikings lived.

## Chapter 2

# Vikings and Fishermen

More than 1000 years ago, Viking settlers from Greenland came to live on the northern tip of Newfoundland. They didn't stay long. No one even knew they had been there until 1960 when **archaeologists** unearthed the remains of their settlement at L'Anse aux Meadows. This name evolved from the French name L'Anse aux Meduses – the bay of jellyfish.

But the Vikings were not the first residents of the region. Aboriginal peoples have made Newfoundland and Labrador their home for thousands of years. Groups whom archaeologists call the Maritime Archaic made campsites and villages along the Labrador coast about 7500 years ago. Researchers are still studying the remains of their settlements. Archaeologists think ancient Arctic peoples, whom they call Palaeo-Eskimos, lived in Newfoundland and Labrador 4000 years ago. The Inuit call these people the Tuniit.

The Thule were the **ancestors** of today's Inuit of Labrador. They arrived from Alaska about 1000 years ago. They survived in the harsh climate by whaling and hunting.

An Inuit hunter, as depicted by a European explorer in 1766

# Innu, Beothuk and Mi'kmaq

The Innu of northern Newfoundland and Labrador were **semi-nomadic** hunters. Caribou was their most important source of food, and they used the hides for clothing, blankets and tent coverings. The Mi'kmaq and the Beothuk lived on the island of Newfoundland. From their communities close to the sea, they fished and hunted sea animals including whales, seals and walruses. They used seal and walrus skins for clothing as well.

Demasduit was one of the last surviving Beothuk. She died in 1820.

When Europeans came to Newfoundland and Labrador in the 1600s, their settlements pushed Aboriginal peoples inland. European diseases killed off entire communities because Aboriginal peoples had no **immunity** to them. Today, there are no longer any Beothuk. Some Mi'kmaq peoples still live on the island. The Innu live in Labrador, as do the Inuit.

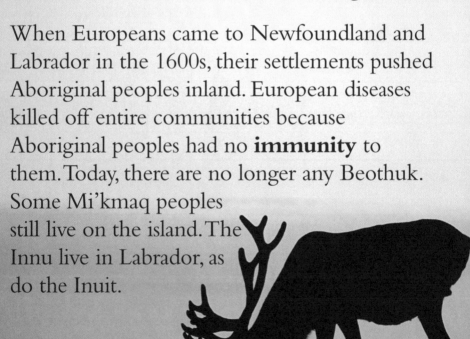

An Innu hunter hangs marten skins in front of his tent at his Labrador camp. Many Innu and Inuit now live in permanent communities but still hunt, fish and trap seasonally.

Aboriginal peoples and European settlers hunted seals and whales for meat and used their skins to make clothing. Whale and seal oil was used as lantern oil. Sealing survives today, although pressure from animal rights groups has threatened it as a way of life.

# Cabot's landing

Five hundred years after the Vikings disappeared from Newfoundland, another European explorer happened upon the island. In 1497 John Cabot landed his ship at Cape Bonavista on a misguided search for spices in Asia. Other European explorers soon followed, mapping and charting the land and its waters.

John Cabot, having crossed the Atlantic from England, greets Aboriginal people at Bonavista.

A replica of Cabot's ship the *Matthew* was built in 1997 for the 500th anniversary of his landing.

# A good catch

The waters surrounding Newfoundland teemed with fish in 1497. Fishing vessels from Europe began to make trips every summer across the Atlantic Ocean to the Grand Banks, off the southeast coast. Reports claimed that the cod were so plentiful they could be scooped from the water in buckets.

Crews from Spain, France and Portugal heavily salted their catches on board ship to prevent rot on the return trip. English crews had less salt, so they set up shore camps, lightly salted and washed the fish and laid it out on wooden platforms called flakes, to dry under the hot sun.

Codfish are cured, or preserved, on outdoor flakes. This method of preserving fish has been used for hundreds of years.

Sir Humphrey Gilbert claims Newfoundland for England despite the presence of Spanish, French and Portuguese fishermen and ship captains in the harbour at St. John's.

# Claiming the land

Fishing was so **profitable** that in 1583, Sir Humphrey Gilbert arrived from England with a **charter** for a permanent settlement in Newfoundland. But he never did start a colony. His ship sank on its return voyage.

From 1610 through the 1620s, several settlements were established by English traders or trading companies. Most were later abandoned when they failed to make money or were besieged by pirates.

The West Country Merchants, a group of English businessmen, controlled the fishing grounds off the coast of Newfoundland. They discouraged permanent settlement because it interfered with seasonal fishing. By 1634 the English established the fishing admiralty. In this system, the captain of the first ship to arrive at a Newfoundland port, or fishing station, was named the fishing admiral. He would control all of the ships, supplies and fishermen there for the season. Many fishing admirals, **sponsored** by the Merchants, burned the homes of settlers.

Cupids, Newfoundland, is the site of the oldest British colony in Canada. It was called Cuper's Cove and began with 40 settlers, led by John Guy, in 1610.

# From colony to province

The fishing admiralty was not successful. Bitter battles between English and French settlers raged over land and fishing territories. On the west coast of the Avalon Peninsula, the French built a small settlement called Plaisance, at present-day Placentia. Irish fishermen set up camps for salting and drying cod in St. John's. The English and the French signed treaties over land rights. In 1763, after the **Seven Years War**, more immigrants from England and Ireland came to settle in

Newfoundland. By 1855 Newfoundland became a self-governing British colony.

In 1867 Ontario, Quebec, Nova Scotia and New Brunswick joined together at **Confederation** to form the new country of Canada. Newfoundland remained a British colony. The people of Newfoundland resisted joining Canada because they felt closer to Britain.

The Great Depression during the 1930s shrunk the market for fish. It left Newfoundland broke, and Britain took direct control of the colony again. By 1946 the pressure to join Canada was great. In 1948 Newfoundlanders took part in two referendums – a vote to determine how people feel about an issue. The question was: should Newfoundland remain a British colony or join Canada in Confederation?

The result was very close, but the people of the province chose Canada. In 1949 a politician named Joseph R. Smallwood was among those who signed the document that officially recognized Newfoundland as the newest province of Canada. Joey Smallwood became the province's first premier.

Joey Smallwood was the colourful premier of Newfoundland for 23 years, from 1949 to 1972.

It's easy to know your neighbour in small outports such as New Bonaventure at Trinity Bay.

## Chapter 3
# Some Shockin' Good

Newfoundlanders love to perform, and they love to laugh. Sharing a song and a story with neighbours has always been important to communities separated by long, lonely distances. **Isolation** makes people come together and creates a strong loyalty to their **heritage**. Some Newfoundlanders and Labradorians feel more closely tied to their ancestors than to other Canadians.

# Island talk

Most people in Newfoundland share an Irish or English background. They have a distinct accent that is described as a lilt. This means that their voices rise and fall in a rhythm as they speak, in a way that sounds a little bit like singing. Labradorians who are Innu or Inuit do not share the same accent. They also have languages of their own, called Innu-aimun and Inuktitut.

Snowmobiles are necessary in remote Labrador communities where there are few roads.

Newfoundlanders not only speak English with a special accent, they have their own vocabulary too. It can be difficult to understand for those who "come from away," as Newfoundlanders call people not from the island. For example, a pancake is called a "gandy," a "hidey-hole" is a cupboard and a "goat" is a neighbour. The term "b'y," a short form of the word boy, is now used to refer to any person, often affectionately.

The Newfoundlander sense of fun and liveliness is also shown in some of their place names: Ha Ha Bay, Joe Batt's Arm, Bacon Cove, Blow Me Down, Bald Head, Maggoty Point and Heart's Content are just a few.

Come By Chance is just one of many colourfully named communities in Newfoundland and Labrador.

Neighbours play traditional music at a "kitchen party."

# Reels and jigs

Singing and playing music are popular pastimes. Traditional fiddle music, which was enjoyed by the first Irish settlers, is still played by Newfoundlanders today.

Tunes known as reels and jigs are great for dancing, and are often played at gatherings in kitchens, living rooms and neighbourhood pubs. Sea shanties are old songs of sailing and fishing that have been passed down through the years. Everyone who knows the words will sing along with the performers.

# Winter fun

Mummering is an old tradition from England that is very much alive in Newfoundland today. Every year around Christmas, people disguise themselves and call on their neighbours. They entertain their hosts with storytelling, music and jokes, and some even perform short plays. The hosts must try to guess who is hiding beneath the mummers' disguises.

(left) A mummer keeps his identity well hidden under a dress and a head covering.

Curling is one of the sports that Newfoundlanders enjoy through the cold, harsh winters. Brad Gushue skipped his team to Olympic gold in 2006.

David Blackwood, a famous printmaker from Newfoundland, has created hundreds of icy-grey depictions of winter on the island.

All aboard! Newfoundland dogs pulled their weight and more through the snow, as this photo from the early 1900s shows.

# Flippers, cheeks and tongues

Since Newfoundland and Labrador is so close to the sea, fish and shellfish are food **staples**. Newfoundlanders are fond of local delicacies that cannot be found anywhere else in Canada. Seal flipper pie is a baked pastry dish with pieces of seal meat. It is not common, but most tourists are eager to give it a try. Cod tongues and cheeks are other delicacies. The squishy, wet tongues are sometimes called "sea kisses" because of their texture. Scrunchions, which are fried pork rinds, are a delicious complement to any dish.

Walking away from a large meal, you might hear a Newfoundlander moan, "I'm blowed up like a harbour tom-cod." This is a delightful way of saying, "I'm stuffed!"

This woman is enjoying seal flipper pie, a Newfoundland treat.

## Chapter 4

# From Land and Sea

For hundreds of years, Newfoundland meant fish. More specifically, it meant cod. When Sir Humphrey Gilbert made his voyage to Newfoundland in 1583, he brought with him a poet who wrote that the waters of Newfoundland yielded "fish without end." The poet was wrong. Even though fishing had been a way of life and a major industry for hundreds of years, in the 1970s cod stocks began to decline.

# Industry collapse

By 1992 the government of Canada shut down the cod fishery, a huge part of the fishing industry. The effect was **devastating**. Many fishers and fishery workers lost their jobs. Thousands moved away to work in other provinces.

Today, many fish processing plants are closed or open only for short periods of time. There are far fewer full-time fishers. Those who remain now catch halibut, crab, lobster and salmon, as well as small amounts of cod, which is strictly regulated.

**Fishers and fish plant workers protest the closing of a processing plant.**

Cod used to be king, but now some fishers make a living from crab or lobster.

Tourism is a big industry in Newfoundland and Labrador. In late spring and early summer, giant icebergs float south from Greenland. The route they take is known as Iceberg Alley. At the same time, migrating whales, including humpbacks, minkes and pilots, also draw tourists to the province.

Iron ore is mined and processed in Labrador City, Labrador.

## Minerals and power

Labrador is one of the leading producers of iron ore. In fact, it has the largest iron ore concentration and yield in North America. Entire settlements were built around the mines in Labrador City and Wabush.

In 1993 prospectors discovered a large nickel deposit in Voisey's Bay, Labrador. Millions of tonnes of nickel are buried in the rocks there. The discovery has led to more prospecting in Labrador.

Nickel is used in brass plating and to make coins and steel.

**33**

Labrador is also a major source of hydroelectric power. Water from the Churchill River is diverted to the Churchill Falls hydroelectric power station. Churchill Falls is the second-largest hydro plant in the world. Most of the energy produced here is sold to the neighbouring province of Quebec.

A hydroelectric dam and dike overlook the Smallwood reservoir in Churchill Falls, Labrador. It was named after former Newfoundland premier Joey Smallwood.

The Hibernia platform thrusts out of the ocean like a concrete and steel island 224 metres high.

## Oil from the sea

Fishermen and whalers once hauled their big catches from the Grand Banks. Today, those waters yield a different treasure: oil and natural gas. The Hibernia oil field, about 320 kilometres from the city of St. John's, is 80 metres beneath the sea. In 1997 a huge oil platform was erected that extracts millions of barrels of oil from the sea each year.

# From the land

Berries thrive in the shallow soil in Newfoundland. Blueberries are the main fruit crop, but also important are tart, red partridgeberries and sweet orange bakeapples. All are excellent for jams and preserves.

Ninety per cent of the province's timber harvest is used in the pulp and paper industry.

## Chapter 5

# Outport Life

In the early settler days of Newfoundland, people lived in small communities next to the ocean. These settlements were called outports. Almost everyone was involved in fishing. Men and boys over the age of thirteen went to sea to fish. Women and younger children stayed ashore to do much of the processing work. This meant cleaning and gutting the fish, and then curing it with salt to prevent it from rotting. Fish were set to dry on platforms called flakes, located near the water.

Every night, and whenever the weather threatened rain, the children brought the fish under shelters. Women ruled the flake. They organized the catch and told the men how much fish to bring back each day. They also kept vegetable gardens near their houses, further up from shore.

"The men catch it and the women make it" is an old Newfoundland saying, meaning women dried or "made" codfish on flakes.

A boy cuts the tongues out of codfish heads as a way of making pocket money. Cod tongues are a delicacy.

# Changing ways

Outports were little worlds unto themselves. Many had just a few houses, a church and a hall. Over time, some of them grew into big villages such as Harbour Grace. Beginning in the 1950s, the provincial government decided to encourage people to move away from outports. Fishing had changed. Larger vessels were operating farther from shore. By the 1970s, more than 220 outport communities had been abandoned. The people were resettled in larger villages and cities, but their way of life was lost.

Villagers worked together to haul a building over ice from an outport to a new location.

## Chapter 6
# Points of Pride

▶ Newfoundland has two UNESCO World Heritage sites: the Viking settlement at L'Anse aux Meadows and Gros Morne National Park (above).

▶ Sir Wilfred Grenfell was a young English doctor who came to Labrador in 1892 on a hospital ship. Shocked by the poor health and harsh life of the people, he stayed to open hospitals in both Labrador and Newfoundland, providing medical care to communities that had none. Today, the International Grenfell Association provides scholarships to students interested in studying medicine.

▶ Chunks of icebergs floating off the coast of Newfoundland are harvested to make bottled water and vodka. The water began as snow that fell on Greenland 10,000 to 15,000 years ago.

▶ In 1919 the world's first non-stop transatlantic airplane flight was made from St. John's to Clifden, Ireland. It took British aviators John Alcock and Arthur Whitten Brown over sixteen hours. They chose St. John's because it is the closest point to Europe from North America.

▶ The world's first transatlantic wireless message was sent in 1901 from Cornwall, England, to Signal Hill in St. John's (below). It was received by Italian inventor Guglielmo Marconi. Today he is known as the father of radio.

# Glossary

**ancestors:** A group of people from whom others are descended

**archaeologists:** Scientists who study ancient and prehistoric people and the way they lived

**charter:** A grant of rights, signed by a king or queen

**Confederation:** The joining of Quebec, Ontario, New Brunswick and Nova Scotia in 1867 to form the Dominion of Canada

**currents:** Flows of water moving in a definite direction

**devastating:** Describes something that stuns or destroys

**glaciers:** Masses of slow-moving, compacted snow and ice

**heritage:** Cultural objects and knowledge passed on from earlier generations

**immunity:** Resistence to a disease that a person is born with or acquires over time after being exposed to it

**isolation:** Separation from other people

**plateaus:** Areas of land that have a flat surface but are raised above other areas around them

**profitable:** Describes something that makes money

**semi-nomadic:** Moving to different locations in some seasons, but staying in one place during others

**Seven Years War:** A European war (1756-1763) involving England, France and their allies that spilled over into North America. At the end of the war, France lost its colonies in North America.

**sponsored:** Supported, often with money

**staples:** Basic items in the normal diet of a person or group